6⁵⁰

Washday

Ruth Thomson

Photographs by Maggie Murray
Illustrations by Sheila Jackson

A & C Black · London

They that wash on Monday have all the week to dry;
They that wash on Tuesday are not much awry;
They that wash on Wednesday there's no need to blame;
They that wash on Thursday wash for shame;
They that wash on Friday wash for need;
They that wash on Saturday – oh, they are sluts indeed!

Acknowledgements

The author and publisher would like to thank the following
people for their invaluable help during the preparation of
this book: Gill Tanner, Mrs Tanner's Tangible History,
Nottingham; Dieter Hopkin, former assistant curator,
Erewash Museum, Ilkeston, Derbyshire; Pamela Sambrook,
curator, and Rosemary Taylor, laundry demonstrator,
Staffordshire County Museum, Shugborough; Gill Selwyn,
schools' liaison officer, Beaumanor Hall, Leicestershire;
Monica Stoppleman; Dr Lynda Measor, Senior Lecturer,
Primary Education, West Sussex Institute of Higher
Education
Photographs by Maggie Murray except for: p8 The Mansell
Collection; p9, 14, 17, 21 Beamish Open Air Museum; p12
Bodleian Library, Oxford, John Johnson Collection; p13
Unilever PLC; p18, 19, 23 (inset) Reckitt Products; p23 (top)
Greater London Photographic Library; p25 Wigan Heritage
Service; p28 Gunnersbury Park Museum, London, W3; p29
Neil Thomson; Cover (inset) Mary Evans Picture Library
Quotations: pages 5 and 15, from Back of Beyond: Life in
Holderness before the First World War, by Alice Markham,
introduction by John Markahm, pub. Highgate Publications,
(Beverley) Limited; pages 14, 15, 16, 19, 21, 22 and 23 from
York memories '*At Home*' Personal accounts of domestic life in
York pub York oral History Project, York Castle Museum, 1987;
Page 14 from Archibald Fenner Brockway, Bermondsey Story,
The life of Alfrecd Salter, pub Allen and Unwin, 1949.

A CIP catalogue record for this book is available
from the British Library

ISBN 0–7136–3183–X

© 1990 A & C Black (Publishers) Limited

Published by A & C Black (Publishers) Ltd
35 Bedford Row, London WC1R 4JH

Filmset by August Filmsetting, Haydock, St Helens
Printed in Belgium by Proost International Book Production

Contents

How is your washing done?

How is the laundry done in your home? Does your family have a washing machine, or take the washing to a launderette? Is there anything which needs to be washed by hand?

Modern washing machines automatically fill with water, wash, rinse and drain, at the turn of a knob.

Your great grandma would be amazed at how simple and speedy washing is nowadays. When she was a child, washing was back-breaking, time-consuming, messy and unhealthy. It was done by women, entirely by hand and was by far the heaviest household job, as this lady from Holderness describes:

'Washday meant really hard work with very simple implements – a wash tub, a dolly tub and a dolly stick, and an old fashioned mangle with wooden rollers. We used no soap powder, just bars of kitchen soap and washing soda.'

The few washing machines that had been invented were hand-operated, which was almost as much hard work as washing by hand.

▲ Basic washing equipment – a dolly tub, a dolly stick, a washboard and a scrubbing brush.

Early washing machines had to be filled with hot water and emptied afterwards.

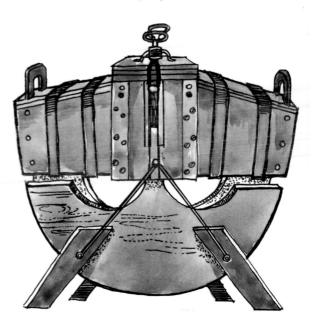

▲ The Faithful Cradle.

◄ The Red Star machine had a mechanised dolly stick. When the big wheel was turned, the stick moved backwards and forwards and pounded the washing.

Time-line

		Great great grandparents were born		Great grandparents were born		
	pre-**1880s**	**1880s**	**1890s**	**1900s**	**1910s**	**1920**
Important events	**1870** Alexander Graham Bell invents telephone	**1888** Dunlop invents pneumatic tyre	**1890** Moving pictures start **1896** First modern Olympic Games	**1901** Queen Victoria dies. Edward VII becomes King **1903** Wright brothers fly first plane	**1910** George V becomes King **1914–18** World War I	**1926** Gen Strike in Britain
Washing dates		**1883** Electric iron patented in United States **1888** First branded soap (Sunlight) sold	**1890** Paraffin iron patented ● Coat hangers begin to be used	**1900** First soapflakes on market **1905** Ironing boards begin to be used **1906** 1 in 10 women in paid work (33% in domestic service) **1907** Invention of tumble drier **1909** Persil first sold in UK	**1911** Average consumption of soap per person per year is 7.4 kg **1917** Electric washing machine introduced in Britain from the United States	**1926** Cen Electricity Board set
Households which had electricity and electric washing machines	100% 80% 60% 40% 20% 0%	electricity				

This time-line shows some of the important events since your great great grandparents were children and some of the events and inventions which have changed the way we do the wash.

Grandparents were born			Parents were born		You were born		
1930s	**1940s**	**1950s**	**1960s**	**1970s**	**1980s**	**1990s**

1936 Edward VIII abdicates. George VI becomes King
● First television broadcasts

1939 World War II starts

1941 Penicillin successfully tested

1945 World War II ends

1947 First supersonic plane

1952 Elizabeth II becomes Queen

EIIR

1959 Yuri Gagarin first man in space

1969 Neil Armstrong – first man on the moon

1973 Britain enters the Common Market

1981 First successful space shuttle flight

1934 Introduction of launderettes

1938 Nylon invented

1939 First (expensive) automatic washing machines

TIDE

1950 Introduction of detergents

1956 First electric spin driers in Britain

1969 'Biological' washing powders introduced

1979 Low lather washing powders for automatic washing machines introduced

1980 Average consumption of soap per person per year is 13.166 kg

electric washing machines

0% 20% 40% 60% 80% 100%

Clothes now and then

Do your everyday clothes look like these? Have a look at the labels inside your clothes, to see what they are made of. Are any of them made of nylon, acrylic, polyester, viscose or jersey? These are artificial fibres, made from chemicals. They are easy to wash and don't need much ironing.

At the beginning of the century when your great grandparents were children, T-shirts and tracksuits, jeans and jumpers, shorts and sweatshirts, didn't exist. All great grandma's clothes were made from natural fibres, such as cotton, wool, linen or silk.

Girls always wore dresses. Their winter dresses were made of wool; their summer dresses were made of cotton. Underneath their dresses they wore a long cotton chemise (a sort of vest), a stiff bodice and several cotton petticoats. In winter, they wore a flannel petticoat for extra warmth.

Well-off men and boys wore suits and waistcoats. Men's best suits were usually black. Boys' suits were usually made of tweed. Both men and boys wore pale shirts with stiff white collars, which could be detached and washed separately.

Poorer families could rarely afford to buy new clothes. They might have had one Sunday-best outfit, but their few everyday clothes were usually patched and mended to make them last as long as possible. Children's clothes were often hand-me-downs or bought second, third or even fourth hand.

▲ Poorer families dressed as respectably as they could afford. Notice how the woman protects her skirt with a large apron.

◀ A well-off family wearing fashionable clothes of the turn of the century.

9

Great grandma's washing

bib

men's cuffs

ladies' cuffs

pinafore

chemise

apron

corset

drawers

socks

cap

These are some of the items you would have found in great grandma's wash. Almost everything that needed frequent washing was made of white cotton or linen. Which of these things do we have today?

A middle class family with children and servants might have had several hundred items to wash at a time. If they could afford it, particularly if the family lived in a town and didn't have much room to dry clothes, they would send their washing to a laundry or employ a washerwoman to come to their house once a fortnight.

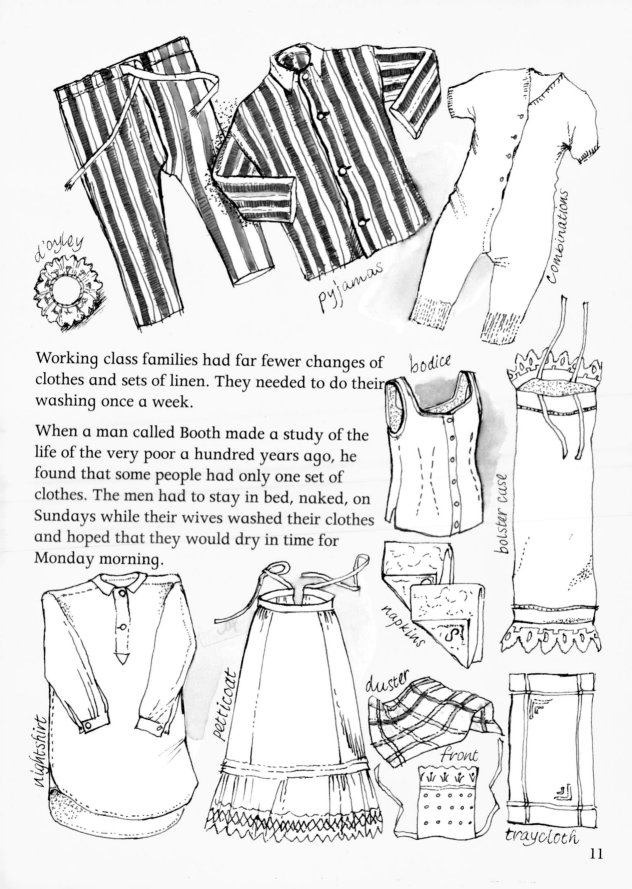

d'oyley

pyjamas

combinations

Working class families had far fewer changes of clothes and sets of linen. They needed to do their washing once a week.

When a man called Booth made a study of the life of the very poor a hundred years ago, he found that some people had only one set of clothes. The men had to stay in bed, naked, on Sundays while their wives washed their clothes and hoped that they would dry in time for Monday morning.

bodice

bolster case

napkins

nightshirt

petticoat

duster

front

traycloth

Clothes care

Very few outer clothes were washable. One of the reasons why people wore so much underwear was to protect their clothes from body dirt. Nonetheless, clothes got stained and dirty.

People took great care to clean clothes as best they could by brushing, sponging or steaming. Household manuals were full of useful tips, such as rubbing stale bread on grease marks, sponging silk with black tea and rubbing velvet with bacon rind! They recommended removers for every possible stain. Rubbing fruit stains with a freshly cut tomato, dipping ink stains in buttermilk and rubbing salt on wine stains were some of their suggestions.

Cleaning tips, taken from ▶ a household manual written at the turn of the century.

▲ Only the very rich could afford to send their clothes to the dry cleaners, which had just started opening in some of the bigger towns.

2721 Cleaning Silk, Satins, Coloured Woollen Dresses &c. — four ounces of soft soap, 4 ounces of honey, the white of an egg & a wineglass of gin. Mix well together & scour the article with a rather hard brush thoroughly; afterwards rinse it in cold water. Leave to drain & iron whilst quite damp.
2722 To Clean Black Cloth Clothes. — Clean the garments well, then boil for

Soap

There were no washing powders or detergents. Washable clothes were cleaned with soap and hot water. The soap was a hard brown lump which people bought, by weight, from a grocer. It was made of tallow (fat) and soda which bleached and wrinkled the skin.

Soap was expensive. People who couldn't afford to buy it made their own. Some country people boiled the leaves of a wild plant, called soapwort, to make a lathery liquid for washing.

During great grandma's childhood, people found new ways to make soap in large quantities and it became cheaper. The first packaged soap was Sunlight, and the first soapflakes were Lux.

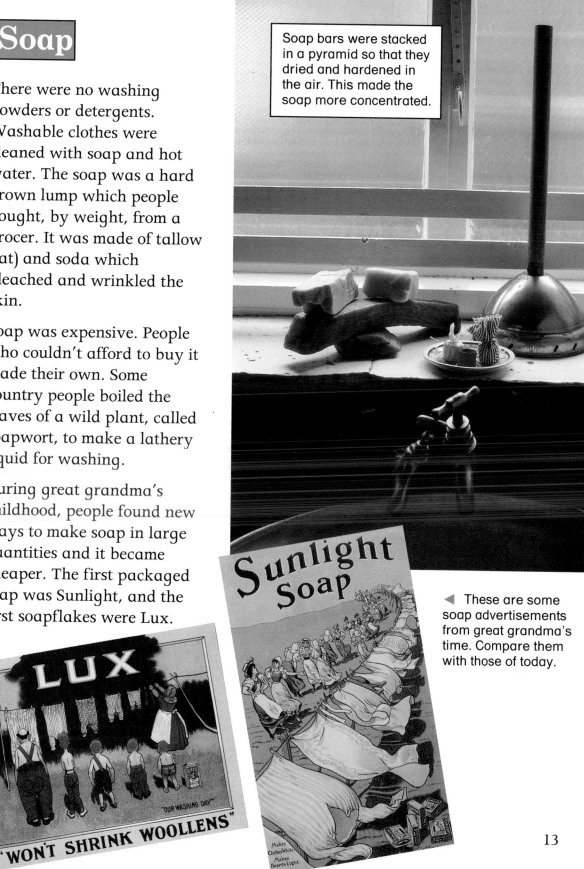

Soap bars were stacked in a pyramid so that they dried and hardened in the air. This made the soap more concentrated.

◄ These are some soap advertisements from great grandma's time. Compare them with those of today.

LUX

"OUR WASHING DAY"

"WON'T SHRINK WOOLLENS"

Sunlight Soap

Makes Clothes White
Makes Hearts Light

13

Water supplies

Getting enough water for cooking, washing and doing the laundry was very hard work. Only big towns had an organised public water supply. Wealthier families had water piped directly to their houses. In poorer areas, families had to fetch water from an outside tap, which they often shared with several other families.

In some places, people had to queue up for their water from a public stand-pipe, pump or fountain. Alfred Salter lived in Bermondsey, London:

'There was one stand-pipe for twenty five houses with the water 'on' for two hours daily, though never on Sundays.'

▲ A typical indoor water pump and stone sink. These can be seen at Erewash Museum, in Ilkeston, Derbyshire.

Carrying water was usually women's ▼ work, but children helped when they were strong enough.

In small villages and out in the country, there was no running water at all. Most houses had a water butt against a wall for catching rainwater that fell from the roof. Some families, like Mrs Burton's, had a well:

'The only water we had was a pump outside with a big well under the wash-house. Every kettle and everything, we'd to go outside, and the water wasn't pure, you know, it was just in a well and it was never cleaned out or anything.'

▲ Large country houses often had their own wells. These children visited Beaumanor Hall, which had a well in its laundry. The children helped to draw some water and tried carrying heavy pails on a yoke. They found it very hard work.

Mrs Markham lived on a farm in East Yorkshire:

'We had a pump for washing and cooking, but all our drinking water had to be fetched by watercart (a large barrel on wheels) from a spring pump two miles away . . . The water from our own pump had a very funny taste and was not suitable for drinking.'

15

Washday

Washing was usually done on a Monday or a Tuesday. It took a whole day, or more if the family was a large one with several servants, and was extremely hard work. To see what the work felt like, these children tried out the equipment used in great grandma's time.

Washday followed a strict routine. The day beforehand, the whites, the coloureds, the flannels and the woollens were sorted into different piles. The whites were soaked in cold water and soap overnight.

These children tried using ▶ a dolly stick and a washboard. They found it took a long time to get anything clean, and the work made their shoulders and backs hurt.

▼ The soap was grated into the water and a handful of soda was added. This softened the water and loosened grease.

Water was fetched from the pump to fill the copper, the metal container in which the water was heated. The fire underneath was laid with sticks, so everything was ready for the next morning. Washday started early as this lady from York remembers:

'Mum used to get up at about six in the morning . . . to light this thing (the copper). There used to be quite a rumpus if it wouldn't go – the sticks were wet . . . or the paper was damp.'

These maids are doing the weekly wash. The one on the left pounds the dirty clothes in a dolly tub, and the one on the right rinses them clean and puts them in the basket in front of her.

Dolly sticks were called different names, depending on where you lived. Peggy legs and dolly maiden were two names. Find out what they were called in your region.

When the water was hot, it was poured into the dolly tub and soap was grated into it. The clothes were put into the tub and churned about with a dolly stick, which looked like a little round stool with a long post fitted to the middle. Can you see how the handle of the dolly stick is twisted to swish the soapy water through the clothes?

Collars and cuffs and any stains were scrubbed against a washboard with a stiff brush and some soap.

17

This girl is ▶ using a copper stick to lift some whites out of the copper.

After being given a good wash, whites were boiled in the copper. Delicate garments were tied in a calico bag to protect them. Boiling was hot work as this woman describes:

'You had to keep poking the whites down with a wooden stick to keep them under the water.'

Rinsing was even worse:

'It was a messy business, filling and emptying the tub until all the soap was gone. There was water all over from lifting the clothes in and out.'

On the last rinse, 'blue' was added to the water; otherwise the soap turned the whites yellow. 'Blue' was a very fine powder, sold in a little linen bag. The bag was dipped into the water and given a quick squeeze. It was important to squeeze in the right amount, as this old lady remembers.

'You cupped the water in your hand to make sure it was the right colour – sky blue. If you put too much in, everything came out blue!'

An old advertisement ▶ for Reckitt's 'blue' bag. You can still buy 'blue' today.

▼ A 'blue' bag.

▼ This rinsing water is a perfect blue. If the 'blue' were not mixed in well, the linen would turn out streaky.

19

The clean washing was put through a mangle to squeeze out the water. Before being mangled, everything was carefully folded edge to edge. Mangling made the linen smooth and glossy so that it didn't need much ironing.

If the weather was fine, clothes were pegged out on a line outside. In towns, people had very little space to hang out their washing. If they did not have a yard, women hung their washing in the street, where it was sometimes knocked down by passing carts. Industrial towns were very polluted. The air was full of smoke and soot which often marked the washing, so some women preferred to dry their clothes indoors.

In this school laundry, ▶ the enormous mangles are mechanically powered. The laundry maids stand on wooden duckboards to keep their feet dry. Where does the water supply come from?

▼ These children are doing the mangling. Two children guide the washing through the mangle, while another turns the handle.

▲ Pegs were larger and stronger than those used nowadays, because fabrics were heavier in great grandma's day.

20

People who lived in the country often laid their washing over hedges or on the grass.

Everyone hated wet washdays.

'Sometimes on a wet day I can remember coming home from school and the place was full – a line down the kitchen, a clothes-horse round the fire, oh golly . . .'

It must have been very damp, smelly and uncomfortable for families who had to wash and dry their washing in the room where they lived and ate.

The children are hanging up the washing in the sunken drying yard at Beaumanor Hall. The yard was walled all round, so that the grand people who lived in the house would not have to see the washing.

When the washing was finished, the copper had to be emptied and scoured and all the equipment had to be scrubbed, rinsed and dried thoroughly, so that it didn't rust.

The next day, there was all the ironing to do. This was almost as much of a chore as the washing.

▶ This child is seeing what it was like to use a flat-iron. She is ironing just as people did then, on a kitchen table covered with a blanket and an old sheet on top.

box iron

flat-iron

box iron

flat-iron

goffering tongs

Mrs Graham explains:

'We'd all those frills and the Lord knows what, to iron. Oh dear! And lots of pin tucks ... old nighties were all pin tucks and the christening gown; all that embroidery anglaise work, every bit.'

Some things, such as tablecloths, pillowcases and aprons were starched before being ironed, to stiffen them and give them a gloss. The starch powder was mixed with cold water to make a paste which was rubbed directly on to collars and cuffs. Other things were dipped in a mixture of starch paste and hot water.

Starch advertisement ▶

▲ Girls had domestic economy lessons at school where they learned how to starch and iron correctly.

Starching helped keep things clean for longer, but it was time consuming. Mrs Graham says:

'Lace curtains, they had to starch those and they were scalloped edged and they had to pummel these until they were right. Some of the gooey starch got stuck, you know...'

Most women used heavy cast iron flat-irons, which they heated on top of their stoves or in front of an open coal fire. They always had a pair of irons.

These were awkward to use, because they did not stay hot for very long. Whilst one was in use, another would be heating. The irons got extremely hot and could only be picked up with a padded holder. To test if they were hot enough to use, women spat on the irons to hear if they sizzled. Worst of all, the fire made irons sooty. They had to be cleaned each time they were used. They were rubbed with sandpaper, coarse salt or bathbrick (a scouring powder) and then wiped clean.

23

This wash-house is at Erewash museum, in Ilkeston. It was taken from a house which was being demolished, and was reconstructed in the museum. It was furnished with the sort of washing equipment which would have been used at the turn of the century.

The wash-house

Women sharing the household washing. You can see the brick wash-house behind them.

Families who lived in small terraced townhouses or country cottages often had a small wash-house, built on to the back of the house. All their washing equipment was kept in here, but if the weather was fine enough women did their washing outside. Imagine how hot, steamy and smelly the wash-house would have been on a wet day.

Look at the big photograph and see if you can spot all the things that were used on washday. Can you see the copper with its lid on, bricked into the corner? The copper was useful for all sorts of things besides washday, such as brewing, boiling puddings and heating bath water.

Mrs Norton remembers bath night:

'We heated water in the copper for bath night. We had our baths in front of the kitchen fire, with the clothes-horse full of clothes pulled round to keep us warm. Us five girls took it in turns to have a bath, all in the same water, mind. I think the cleanest went in first.'

The stone sink was used for scrubbing clothes in, but not for rinsing them. Can you see why? Where do you think the water supply is?

What can you see heating on the range in the fireplace? The lavender hanging above it kept the room smelling fresh.

25

A country house laundry

Big country houses had their own laundries, built well out of sight of the main house. They had two enormous rooms like these; one for washing and the other for drying and ironing.

The rich people who lived in the house changed their clothes several times a day, used towels only once and gave grand dinners where dozens of napkins and serving cloths and several tablecloths were used at one meal.

So much linen was used every day, that this laundry needed to employ three full-time laundrymaids as well as extra help from local village women. The laundrymaids worked six days a week from 7 o'clock in the morning until 7 o'clock at night to get through a week's washing.

Most of the equipment used by the laundrymaids was very similar to the kind used by ordinary working people, although on a much larger scale. But unlike working people, a family like this one had water piped to the house. Soap was bought by the ton and stored in the big wooden chest, until it was needed.

The washing and drying ▶ rooms at Shugborough Hall in Staffordshire look almost as they would have looked at the turn of the century. The rooms have been restored and filled with old washing equipment and linen.

Imagine pulling up the enormous drying rack full of wet clothes. It was so heavy, that it took two laundrymaids to work the pulley.

The box mangle in the centre of the room was used for pressing linen. The laundrymaids wound sheets round rollers and put them under the box, which was full of stones. When the mangle was turned, the box moved over the rollers and its weight smoothed and polished the linen. The mangle was too heavy for the laundrymaids to use. An odd-job man came once a week to turn it for them.

The ironing was done on the big tables all round the room. Can you spot the iron stove, which could heat dozens of flat-irons at once?

Laundries

In some big towns, wealthier people could send their washing out to hand-laundries. The washing was collected from their houses on Monday and returned at the end of the week.

These laundries had few machines. Washing was done in the same way as in homes, but on a much larger scale. The heavy washing and mangling was done by men. Clothes were pounded in enormous wooden tubs, boiled in huge 360 litre coppers and mangled through box mangles.

Laundry workers worked 12 hours a day with two short breaks for meals. Their wages were low and paid partly in beer. The laundries were unhealthy places to work. They were hot and damp because they were usually poorly aired and drained.

By the turn of the century, more modern steam-laundries began and these gradually replaced hand-laundries. Delicate garments were still hand-washed but everything else was washed and mangled by machine, although most ironing was still done by hand.

Dozens of women were employed in this steam laundry to do the starching and ironing by hand.

Washing then and now

▲ This woman is doing her washing at a sink in the back-yard of her house, in Mexico.

In richer, industrialised countries, machines and piped water supplies have made washing clothes a much easier job than it was during great grandma's childhood.

In countries where water supplies are inadequate or where machines are too expensive for most people to afford, washing is still a heavy and time-consuming task.

Compare this modern picture with those on pages 17 and 25. What is different and what is still the same?

How to find out more

Start here	To find out about	Who will have
Old people	Washday in the past	Memories of washday in their childhood. Photographs showing the clothes people wore and possibly some old clothes and linen
● Junk shops ● Second-hand bookshops ● Specialist old clothes shops	Old things to buy	● Washing equipment eg washboards, dolly sticks, pegs, baskets etc. ● Old magazines with advertisements, books on household management, etc. ● Old clothes and linen
Local museums	Washday displays to look at and possibly to handle	Displays of clothes and/or washday equipment you can look at. Handling collections of objects you can touch and use. Reconstructed wash-houses and laundries, with equipment from the turn of the century
Local libraries	● Loan collections ● Reference collections ● Local history section ● Information desk	● Books to borrow ● Books, magazines, newspapers and guides to look at in the library ● Photographs of local people and buildings. Local documents and tapes of local people talking ● Information on how to further your research – useful addresses, guide books, additional reference material
Manufacturers of washing machines, soap and washing powders	History of their products	Booklets, pictures, advertisements and information about the history of their washday products

Who can tell you more?

They can. Record their memories on a tape recorder. Label any clothes, photos or objects lent to you with the name of the owner, and look after them with great care

Specialist shopkeepers often know a lot about their stock and can answer your questions. They may also tell you where to go for further research

- The curator or the museum's education officer or the washing demonstrator
- Look in the museum's bookshop for relevant publications and on the noticeboard or at the information desk for leaflets advertising other museums

- The librarian
- The reference librarian

- Ask the archivist for the name and address of the local history society

The Public Relations Officer of the company, part of whose job is to help with queries like yours

Places to visit

The following places have original or reconstructed wash-houses. Those starred * also have laundry demonstrations either for schools and/or the public. Write to them for further details.

Auchindrain, Inveraray, Argyll, PA32 8XN. Tel: 04995 235
Avoncroft Museum of Buildings, Stoke Heath, Bromsgrove, Worcestershire. Tel: 0527 31363
Barony Chambers Museum, The Cross, Kirkintilloch, Glasgow. Tel: 041 775 1185
Beningbrough Hall, York YO6 1DD. Tel: 0904 470666
Bygones at Holkham, Holkham Park, Wells-next-to-the-sea, Norfolk. Tel: 0328 710806
The Castle Street Georgian House, Chester, Cheshire. Tel: 0244 321616
Easton Farm Park, Wickham Market, Suffolk. Tel: 0728 746475
Elvaston Castle Museum, The Working Estate, Elvaston Castle Country Estate, Borrowash Lane, Elvaston DE7 3EW. Tel: 0332 71342
Erewash Museum, High Street, Ilkeston, Derbyshire. Tel: 0602 303361
Erdigg, near Wrexham, Clwyd, North Wales, LL13 0YT. Tel: 0978 355314
Gwent Rural Life Museum, The Malt Barn, New Market Street, Usk. Tel: 029 132 3777
Hill of Tarvit, nr Cupar, Fife, Scotland. Tel: 0334 53127
Gustav Holst Birthplace Museum, 4 Clarence Road, Pittville, Cheltenham. Tel: 0242 524846
* *Museum of East Anglian Life*, Stowmarket, Suffolk 1P14 1DL. Tel: 0449 612229
* *North Holderness Museum of Village Life*, 11 Newbegin, Hornsea. Tel: 040 12 3430 or 3443
* *Shugborough*, Milford, nr. Stafford ST17 0XB. Tel: 0889 881388
Social History Museum, Holy Trinity Church, Trinity Street, Colchester, Essex. Tel: 0206 712491
* *Somerset Rural Life Museum*, Abbey Farm, Chilkwell Street, Glastonbury BA6 8DB. Tel: 0548 32903
Summerlee Heritage Centre, West Canal Street, Coatbridge ML5 1QD. Tel: 0236 31261
Mrs Tanner's Tangible History, 9 Selby Road, West Bridgeford, Nottingham N92 7BP. Tel: 0602 812039 (visits schools with her own equipment to give demonstrations and workshops).
Welsh Folk Museum, St Fagans, Cardiff CF5 6XB Tel: 0222 569441
Wigan Pier, Wigan WN3 4EU. Tel: 0946 323666

These places have old washday equipment on display:

Abbot Hall, Kendal, Cumbria LA9 5AL. Tel: 0539 22464
Bedford Museum, Castle Lane, Bedford. Tel: 0234 53323
Cookworthy Museum, The Old Grammar School, 108 Fore Street, Kingsbridge, Devon. Tel: 0548 3235
Costworld Countryside Collection, Fosse Way, Northleach. Tel: 0451 60715
Dumfries Museum, The Old Bridge House, Mill Road Dumfries. Tel: 0387 53374
Gloucester Folk Museum, 99–103 Westgate Street, Gloucester GL1 2PG. Tel: 0452 26467
Great Yarmouth Museums, Elizabeth House Museum, 4 South Quay, Great Yarmouth NR30 2QH. Tel: 0493 855746

Gunnersbury Park Museum, Gunnersbury Park, London W3 8LQ. Tel: 01–992 1612
Hawick Museum and Art Gallery, Wilton Lodge Park, Hawick, Scotland. Tel: 0450 73457
Kelso Museum, Turret House, Abbey Court, Kelso, Scotland. Tel: 0573 25470
Museum of English Rural Life, University of Reading, Whiteknights, Reading RG6 2AG.
North Cornwall Museum and Gallery, The Clease, Camelford, Cornwall. Tel: 0840 212954
Powysland Museum, Salop Road, Welshpool, Wales. Tel: 0938 4759
The Tenement House, 145 Buccleuch Street, Garnethill, Glasgow G3 6QN. Tel: 041–333 0183
Wigan Pier, Wigan WN3 4EU. Tel: 0942 323666
Woolstaplers Hall Museum, High Street, Chipping Camden, Gloucestershire. Tel: 0386 840289
York Castle Museum, York YO1 1RY. Tel: 0904 653611

Index